Edited by Peter Cagney

Positively the Last Irish Joke Book

With additional material by
Ernest Forbes

Futura
Macdonald & Co
London & Sydney

A Futura Book

First published in Great Britain by
Futura Publications Limited in 1979
Reprinted 1979, 1980, 1981 (twice), 1982, 1983

ISBN 0 7088 1537 5

Printed in Great Britain by
Hazell Watson & Viney Ltd
Aylesbury, Bucks

Futura Publications
A Division of
Macdonald & Co (Publishers) Ltd
Maxwell House
74 Worship Street
London EC2A 2EN

Paddy said he didn't need a lunch as he was going to buy a lunchtime edition of the *Daily Telegraph*.

* * *

First Irish Farmer: 'My cow fell down a hole and I had to shoot it.'
Second Irish Farmer: 'Did you shoot it in the hole?'
First Irish Farmer: 'No, in the head.'

* * *

Paddy's mother was distressed when she heard he had called his newly born daughter Hazel.
'Holy Saint Patrick,' she cried. 'A saint for every day in the year and he has to call his daughter after a nut.'

* * *

Young Shaun: 'Ma, will you buy me an encyclopaedia?'
Mother: 'That I won't. You'll walk to school like the rest of the children.'

* * *

Murphy's wife telephoned Paddy and told him her husband had a bad case of laryngitis.
'Well, tell him to bring it along to the party tonight. We'll drink anything,' replied Paddy.

* * *

Bridget: 'I hear your husband has given up his clerk's job at the bank.'
Josie: 'That's right. He couldn't stand sitting all day.'

*   *   *

What footwear does Bridget wear when she goes on holiday?
Sling-back wellies.

*   *   *

Paddy was offered the winner of The Grand National but he refused it as he said he had no place to keep it.

*   *   *

'That fella,' said Mrs O'Hara, 'could start a fight in an empty church.'

*   *   *

Mick: 'Was he ill long?'
Paddy: 'No, he died in the best of health.'

*   *   *

Paddy was shaving when he knocked the mirror off the shelf and it fell to the floor and it cracked across the middle.
Paddy gazed at it in horror.
'Bejabber, I've cut my throat,' he gasped.

*   *   *

6

An old Irishman was huddled against the cold and a friendly lady stopped to give him some well-meaning advice.
Lady: 'Why don't you button your coat if you're cold.'
Man: 'No buttons.'
Lady: 'Do you want a pin?'
Man: 'Shure a pin won't keep me warm.'

* * *

'You know,' said Mrs O'Toole, 'you could really feel the heat of that coat the minute you took it off.'

* * *

'What's that new man like?' asked the foreman.
'Ah, he's as good as a man short,' replied Paddy.

* * *

Paddy claims that his wife is the only person in the world who parks her car by ear.

* * *

'You know,' said Paddy in a reflective mood, 'the happiest parents are those without children.'

* * *

Paddy stopped following Manchester United as he said it was a waste of good toilet rolls.

* * *

Paddy: 'Hi, waiter. This fly in my soup is cold.'

* * *

The large car glided to a halt and the American visitor lowered the window and beckoned to Paddy.
'Say, do you know the way to Dublin?'
'Indeed I do, sor,' said Paddy as he walked away.

* * *

'In my day,' said Paddy, 'all them plastic shoes was made of leather.'

* * *

'I don't think our Mick's a bit well,' observed Moira to her friend, 'he's gone for a walk four nights running.'

* * *

'It's been a long day,' complained Mrs Fitzgerald, 'and I haven't sat down since I got up.'

* * *

Said Paddy: 'The best view you can have of Belfast is through the rear window of a car.'

* * *

Mrs O'Neill was outraged. 'You know that Paddy fella? Well, he put his head through the winda and me sittin' in the middle of my tea.'

* * *

'Well, you know,' said Paddy, 'I don't mind what the weather's like as long as it's warm and sunny.'

*　　*　　*

And if you're in Ballymena and say 'passion' they'll think you're telling them it's raining.

*　　*　　*

Irish alibi: To be in two places at the same time.

*　　*　　*

Irish undertaker knocking on door: 'Is this where the dead man lives?'
Reply from inside: 'No, three doors up.'

*　　*　　*

Paddy had just got a job in a large London hotel and he was told to go and make fifty beds, so he asked where he would get the wood, hammer and nails.

*　　*　　*

Paddy looked at Bridget's ring.
'Eighteen carats?' he asked.
'No, onions. I've just had a hamburger.'

*　　*　　*

The foreman walked up to Paddy who was sitting on a workbench eating his lunch.
Foreman: 'Oi, where's your mate?'
Paddy: 'Between me bread.'

*　　*　　*

Paddy and Mick went to a football match. At the turnstile Mick asked for one and a half.
'Who's the half for?' demanded the gateman.
'Paddy here,' replied Mick. 'He can only see one team.'

*　　*　　*

Paddy has gone on a mountaineering expedition to Russia where he intends to climb the Urinals.

*　　*　　*

Paddy thought his navel was just a place to keep salt in when he was eating hard-boiled eggs in bed.

*　　*　　*

Paddy: 'I think I'll take Angie Dickinson out again.'
Mick: 'Have you taken her out before?'
Paddy: 'No, but I've thought about it before.'

*　　*　　*

A member of an Irish rugby team went home one day with a badly bruised and cut ear.
'Aren't you worried?' asked his mother.
'Indeed I am. I don't even know whose ear it is,' came the reply.

* * *

Paddy was caught stealing a calendar and got twelve months.

* * *

Old Patrick stopped cutting the hedge as the big car drew up beside him and an English visitor enquired, 'Could you tell me the way to Balbriggan, please?'
Patrick wiped his brow.
'Certainly, sor. If you take the first road to the left . . . no still that wouldn't do . . . drive on for about four miles then turn left at the crossroads . . . no that wouldn't do either.'
Patrick scratched his head thoughtfully. 'You know, sor, if I was going to Balbriggan I wouldn't start from here at all.'

* * *

Paddy got a box of crackers for Christmas, now he's looking for the cheese.

* * *

Mick: 'I hear that Rory Flynn got married.'
Paddy: 'Good! I never did like that fella.'

* * *

When Paddy wrote his first book the publisher suggested he should choose a pen name so he called himself Ball Point.

*　　*　　*

When Mick arrived in China he asked if anyone knew an Irishman called Paddy Fields.

*　　*　　*

Paddy was rather sad after seeing the body of a dead atheist.
'There he was. All dressed up and no place to go.'

*　　*　　*

Paddy couldn't understand why he should back a horse each way as he thought he was smart enough to know that a horse only ran forward.

*　　*　　*

When Paddy was asked if he had a criminal record he replied, 'No, only one of Dean Martin.'

*　　*　　*

Paddy was very disappointed when he joined the MCC and found that maidens, fine legs and a tickle between the legs were all terms used in cricket.

*　　*　　*

Paddy: 'My sister has married an Englishman with a bad leg called Fred.'

* * *

Mrs O'Keefe: 'Is it possible to insure my husband? He has two wooden legs.'
Agent: 'What kind of insurance – life, fire or theft?'

* * *

When Paddy bought a used car he checked it and found the lights didn't light, the starter didn't start, the wipers didn't wipe and the pistons completely confused him.

* * *

Paddy couldn't wash his face at the hotel as there was only a hand towel in the bathroom.

* * *

Paddy refused to go on blind dates as he said he had perfect eyesight.

* * *

Paddy always fished under the bridge when it was raining as he figured the fish would shelter there.

* * *

The Irish cricketer died and went to heaven. At the gates he was asked if there was anything he wished to tell. 'Well, to tell the truth there is something which has plagued me for years.'

'And what is that, my son?'

'Some years ago when Ireland played the MCC at Lords I opened the innings for Ireland and I survived an appeal for caught at first slip and I knew I had touched the ball but I stayed on and scored 295.'

'Did Ireland win?' asked the saint.

'Yes, we won by an innings and 27 runs.'

'Think nothing about it, my son, all is forgiven. Enter the gates.'

The cricketer was delighted.

'Oh, thank you, Saint Peter.'

'By the way, I'm not Peter. I'm St Patrick,' smiled the saint.

*   *   *

Paddy got so fed up reading that smoking was bad for his health that he immediately gave up reading.

*   *   *

Paddy was given a fire guard and now he's looking for a fire that burns on one side only.

*   *   *

For those of you who want to get away from smoking, try the new Irish cigarette – it has a six-inch filter.

*   *   *

When Paddy found a pipe in the bedroom he thought his wife had given up smoking cigarettes.

*   *   *

When Paddy was laying concrete in a hurry he mixed the cement with quick sand.

*   *   *

'Ah it was a lovely dress,' said Maureen, 'and it would have fitted me if I could have got into it.'

*   *   *

Paddy really enjoys a joke. So much that he usually laughs at each joke three times. The first time when somebody else gets it. The second time a week later when he gets it and the third time a month later when someone explains it to him.

*   *   *

Paddy met a girl who was one of twins.
'Hello der. Now tell me, is it you or your sister? Shure each of you looks so like both of you that I can't tell looking at you whether it's you or the other one.'

*   *   *

In an Irish court a female nudist accused a male nudist of getting her drunk and trying to drape her.

*   *   *

Paddy went into a second-hand shop to buy one for his watch.

* * *

Paddy has come to the conclusion that modern paintings are signed at the bottom so you can hang them the right way up.

* * *

When Paddy was told that the eunuchs of Saudi Arabia had gone on strike he exclaimed, 'Good for them. What have they got to lose?'

* * *

The secretary of the Irish Teachers' Union said that the teaching profession in Ireland was so tough when a pupil raised his hand the teacher didn't know whether he wanted to leave the room or had a gun in his back.

* * *

Mickey Flynn who failed to swim the English Channel blames his trainer who he claims, 'Put so much grease on me I kept slipping out of the water.'

* * *

At the opening of the London production of 'Hello, Hollywood' Paddy thought the show was so bad that he asked the lady sitting in front of him to put her hat on.

*   *   *

Poor Paddy! He was caught red-handed stealing a drum of yellow paint!

*   *   *

Sign in an Irish pub:
'This establishment closes at 11 o'clock sharp. We are open from 10 a.m. until 11 p.m. and if you haven't had enough to drink at that hour the management feel you haven't really been trying.'

*   *   *

Paddy thinks the best way of getting rid of the noise in his car is to let her drive.

*   *   *

Paddy was told not to come back to night school. It appears that he put his hand up to leave the room and the lady teacher told him to stick it out till break – and he did!

*   *   *

A rule in an Irish nudist camp is that members must wear a coloured tape around their wrists to distinguish the men from the women.

*　　*　　*

Paddy was walking through a graveyard when he came across a headstone with the inscription 'Here lies a politician and an honest man.'
'Faith now,' exclaimed Paddy, 'I wonder how they got the two of them in the one grave.'

*　　*　　*

Mick had been convicted at least twenty times before.
'Sor,' he said, 'I would like to have my case postponed for a month. My lawyer is ill.'
'But you were caught in the act of stealing. What could your lawyer possibly say in your defence?'
'Exactly, sor, that's what I'm anxious to know.'

*　　*　　*

Priest: 'I am pleased, Patrick, to see you have given up drinking on a Saturday night.'
Pat: 'Oh, is that where I was?'

*　　*　　*

Paddy was late for the performance and as he tried to find his seat in the front row someone shouted: 'Sit down in the front.'
To which Paddy replied: 'I can't. I don't bend that way.'

*　　*　　*

An Irish drill sergeant was teaching a class of recruits how to use their parachutes.
'What happens if the parachute doesn't open?' asked one young soldier.
'Dat, me boyo, is what is known as jumping to a conclusion.'

* * *

When Mick was asked if he had seen any picnickers he replied he hadn't but had spotted some blue knickers on a clothesline.

* * *

When Bridget saw the graffito 'Make love not war', she scribbled her telephone number underneath.

* * *

Shamus was getting irate and shouted upstairs to his wife, 'Hurry up or we'll be late.'
'Oh, be quiet,' replied his wife. 'Haven't I been telling you for the last hour that I'll be ready in a minute?'

* * *

Miss Kathleen Brennan who appeared in a bankruptcy court in Dublin stated whilst she was a top Irish model she only made a bare living.

* * *

In a Dublin court the case was dismissed of a labourer claiming compensation for injuries received when struck on the head by a falling hammer. The judge said that as he wasn't wearing a safety helmet at the time he hadn't a leg to stand on.

* * *

The Irish people rejoiced when they heard the Pope encourage mixed marriages – one man and one woman.

* * *

An Irish army officer who was inspecting the guard came across a very raw-looking soldier.
'What are you here for?' he asked.
'To report anything unusual, sor.'
'What would you call usual?'
'Dat I don't know, sor.'
'What would you do if you saw the British Navy sailing up the River Liffey?'
'Sign the pledge, sor.'

* * *

Mick: 'How long did it take your wife to learn to drive?'
Pat: 'Oh, tree or four.'
Mick: 'Weeks?'
Pat: 'Cars.'

* * *

An item in an Irish newspaper on the m[?]
man called O'Hagan.
'The murderer was evidently after money[?]
Mr O'Hagan had deposited all his money in the ba[nk]
the day before so he lost nothing but his life.'

*　　*　　*

Paddy thought the Spanish Armada had failed because
it couldn't do enough miles to the galleon.

*　　*　　*

Paddy was directing his first play and was not satisfied
with the hero's dying scene.
'Come on,' he cried, 'put more life into your dying.'

*　　*　　*

Now an SOS for the deep sea divers of the Irish Oil
Rig in the North Sea . . . come up at once, your rig is
sinking.

*　　*　　*

A Dublin bank manager reports that he received a
telephone call from a man who said, 'This is a stick-
up! Post £1,000 to Mick Malone, 2b, Liffey Road,
Dublin.'

*　　*　　*

And then of course there was the Irishman who tried
to tunnel his way out of a prison ship.

*　　*　　*

23

Teacher: 'Who was the first woman?'
Paddy: 'Being a gentleman, sor, I can't tell.'

*   *   *

Irish Father: 'What is your reason for wanting to marry my daughter?'
Irish Suitor: 'I have no reason. I'm in love.'

*   *   *

Priest to a head-bandaged O'Casey: 'I'm going to pray that you forgive Ryan for throwing that brick at you.'
O'Casey: 'Spare your prayer, Father, till I get better, then pray for Ryan.'

*   *   *

The judge looked at the burly Irishman and asked: 'Well what do you plead? Guilty or not guilty?'
The Irishman looked at the judge and growled: 'Figure it out for yourself, that's what's you're getting paid for.'

*   *   *

Bridget to her husband in bed: 'You go ahead and read, dear, I'm going to put the light out and go to sleep.'

*   *   *

At the Irish Olympics the winner of the 1500-metre hurdles was accused of taking stimulants before the race and an objection was made by other contestants. However, the objection was dismissed when the judges were informed that the winner Joe O'Neill had eaten 5 pounds of peas immediately before the event in an effort to get a following wind.

* * *

How do you know an Irish gardener?
He's the one watering the garden during a rainstorm.
How do you know an intelligent Irish gardener?
He's the one holding an umbrella while watering the garden during a rainstorm.

* * *

NEWS ITEM
Irish exporters claim that the demand for the Irish digital watch has broken all records.
It is a new type of watch – when you press the button, a little red arrow appears pointing to the nearest pub.

* * *

Judge: 'And so this is the fifth person you've knocked down this year.'
Paddy: 'Dat's not true, sor. One of them was the same person twice.'

* * *

Today the president of Eire laid a wreath on the grave of Patrick Flynn, Ireland's unknown soldier.

As a publican Patrick Flynn was well known, but as a soldier he was unknown.

*   *   *

The woman was in bed with her lover and had just told him how stupid her Irish husband was when the door was thrown open by a six foot seven, eighteen-stone Irishman. He glared at the lover and bellowed: 'What are you doing?'

'There,' said the wife, 'didn't I tell you he was stupid!'

*   *   *

An unknown sailor is in a Dublin hospital suffering from three bullet wounds. He is expected to recover from two of them.

*   *   *

Then there was the cross-eyed Irish teacher who resigned because he had no control over his pupils.

*   *   *

And what do you think about the lion escaping from the circus in Belfast? The police and army personnel who chased it were all armed but had orders not to shoot it in the stomach in case they hit the lion-tamer.

*   *   *

NEWS ITEM

The Rev. Ian Paisley has made a record on which he sings in praise of the Roman Catholic Church. The record will be issued as a single, under an Orange label and without a hole in the middle.

*　　*　　*

The Secretary of State for Northern Ireland is going to try and stop the smuggling of cattle and pigs across the border and police are having some success already. Only last night they caught three Irishmen on the border. Two of the men were each carrying a pig and the third had nine piglets under his coat.

One man explained he was simply carrying home the bacon, the second said he was taking home a little something for his daughter's piggy-bank whilst the man with the piglets pointed out he was a postman and was delivering a litter.

*　　*　　*

Did you hear about the Irishman who went to Vernons as he wanted to learn to swim?

*　　*　　*

On the sounding of the alarm to indicate a prison break-out at one of Ireland's top security prisons, police and soldiers converged on the entrance door whilst twenty prisoners escaped through the exit door.

*　　*　　*

'Tell me, Patrick, how did you manage to get so very drunk last night?' asked the parish priest.
'Well you see, Father, it was like this. I got into very bad company after winning a bottle of whiskey at a raffle.'
'But you were with Mick Mulligan, Shaun O'Toole and Peter Ryan and they don't drink.'
'Dat's what I mean, Father.'

* * *

'Are you sure,' an anxious patient asked an Irish doctor, 'that I will recover? I have heard that doctors sometimes give wrong diagnoses and have treated patients for pneumonia who afterwards died of typhoid fever.'
'Have no fear, madam. If I treat you for pneumonia you'll die of pneumonia,' assured the doctor.

* * *

Michael Kennedy, an Irish photographer, was arrested in the Hollywood home of Angie Dickinson last night. He explained to the police he thought Miss Dickinson had the most wonderful pair of legs in the world and he was determined to get a photograph of her legs or bust.

* * *

Peace seems to be returning to Northern Ireland.
Two hundred milk-float tail gunners have just received their discharge papers.

* * *

And what about the Irish Kamikazi pilot who has just been awarded the Silver Star for completing twenty-five successful missions?

*   *   *

'Ma, there's a strange man at the door.'
'Holy Saint Patrick! Has he got a bill?'
'No, ma, just an ordinary red nose.'

*   *   *

'You know you're the first girl I've ever kissed,' said Paddy as he changed gear with his knees.

*   *   *

In England it is quite common for a doctor to have a reputation for being a lady killer but in Ireland doctors don't make any distinction between the sexes.

*   *   *

Now for readers who are interested in boat racing.
In the Ladies' Coxless Four Race on the river Shannon today the Ladies of Dublin beat the Ladies of Cork.
It was a very close finish as there wasn't a length between them.

*   *   *

And did you hear about the Irish policeman who got his bicycle stolen while he was pushing it home?

*   *   *

In view of contraceptives being banned in Eire the government has published a book called *Birth Control by the Book Method*. Once having bought the book the woman should hold it tightly between her knees . . . and keep it there.

*   *   *

He gazed down at his first born. Wonder and amazement were reflected on his face.
Maria slipped an arm around his waist and said softly, 'What are you thinking, Paddy?'
'How do dey make a cradle like that for only four pounds,' replied Paddy.

*   *   *

NEWS ITEM
We regret to announce the death of Mick Flynn, the leading Irish water polo player who was drowned when he fell off his pony.

*   *   *

And what about the little old Irish lady who was too frightened to fly so she always travelled by bus until one day an aeroplane crash landed on it.

*   *   *

Poor Paddy went to the dentist to get a wisdom tooth put in.

*   *   *

'When the man stole your watch why didn't you chase him?' asked the policeman.

'I couldn't,' replied Paddy. 'I hadn't the time.'

*   *   *

In a small town in County Antrim, a local company staged the play 'Murder in the Old Red Barn'.

The audience was very meagre and as the villain dragged the heroine down stage to the footlights he hissed in her ear: 'Are we alone?'

'No, mac,' interrupted the lone occupant of the hall, 'not tonight, but you will be tomorrow night.'

*   *   *

Michael O'Malley has won the title of Ireland's most honest farmer because he packed all the small apples at the top of the barrels . . . then marked them 'Open Other End.'

*   *   *

And we regret to announce the death of Patrick Flynn who left Dublin last night to walk around the world. He was drowned in the Irish Sea.

*   *   *

In Belfast last night a gang of twenty terrorists was caught by soldiers on routine patrol. Three of the terrorists were caught by the sergeant, five by corporals and the rest by the privates.

*   *   *

NEWS ITEM

Now some good news for pianists who can't read music.
The Irish Piano Company have produced a piano with a vertical keyboard for those who play by ear.

* * *

NEWS ITEM

Patrick O'Toole, the Irish balloonist who left Dublin yesterday to fly across the Atlantic Ocean was today sighted over France.
In a radio message he stated the fault lay with his ground staff who pointed him in the wrong direction.

* * *

Shamus raved at his wife.
'Did you ever take time to think if you've got a brain?'
'Certainly not,' retorted Maureen, 'such a thing would never enter my head.'

* * *

NEWS ITEM

An Irishman appeared in a Belfast court today charged with assault against his ex-girlfriend when he cello-taped her breasts together. He pleaded not guilty, claiming he was following a well-known practice: 'If you can't lick 'em, join 'em.'

* * *

33

NEWS ITEM

In a Dublin court today an Irishman was charged with contempt when he made rude faces at the judge with his fingers.

*　　*　　*

NEWS ITEM

An official at an Irish nudist camp stated today that camp life was not only healthy but it was also educational as one male member on joining the camp could only count up to twenty but can now count to twenty-one.

*　　*　　*

NEWS ITEM

In a Dublin court today an Irishman pleaded guilty to being drunk in charge. He said he had left a party early because he had been too drunk to sing.

*　　*　　*

NEWS ITEM

Irish miners were very excited to-day when they unearthed what they thought was the world's largest diamond in the diamond fields of County Down. However, they were disappointed when experts stated their find was a shamrock.

*　　*　　*

NEWS ITEM

And next week we'll be talking to an Irish company director who thinks that a permanent secretary is one who is screwed on the desk.

*　　*　　*

NEWS ITEM

Mrs Sarah Donnelly, a Dublin housewife who has given birth to her twelfth child, says she has had her feet in the stirrups more times than John Wayne.

*　　*　　*

. . . and now oil. The director of The Irish Sea Oil Drilling Company sent the manager of one of the oil rigs a 'Get Well Quick' card.

And on the subject of oil this company has produced 100 barrels a day for the last month . . . no oil . . . just barrels.

*　　*　　*

In a Belfast Court today a woman who wanted a divorce on the grounds of cruel treatment was asked by the magistrate why she referred to her husband as 'Beans' and she replied it was because he knew fifty-seven ways.

*　　*　　*

A man was treated in a Belfast hospital tonight for a broken nose, a fractured jaw and a black eye.

He received the injuries when fighting for his girl friend's honour. But it appeared she wanted to keep it.

*　　*　　*

At a court in Tipperary an Irish motorist stated that he drove into a tree to avoid having an accident.

*　　*　　*

And in Belfast a well-known shop has advertised a Big
Bomb Sale – so do hurry if you want a big bomb.

*   *   *

And now here's some good news for people who like to
combine outdoor and indoor sports – Irish Cinemas
Ltd are installing swimming pools in all their cinemas
for those doing the breast stroke in the back row.

*   *   *

Heard on Belfast Radio:
We wish to correct a news item read earlier on this
programme which, due to a typing error, was incorrect.
The item should have read 'a man in Ballymena was
struck by lightning while he was washing his walls'.

*   *   *

In a national survey recently carried out in Ireland
husbands were asked the question:
'Do you talk to your wife when you are making love?'
50% said they did not
20% said yes
25% said sometimes
4% said they couldn't recall
and
1% said only if there was a telephone convenient.

*   *   *

The train slowly made its way to Cork and the two travellers had plenty of time to get to know each other.
First Man: 'Are you going to the hall where Cavan O'Connor is making a speech?'
Second Man: 'Indeed I am.'
First Man: 'Well, I wouldn't bother if I were you for they tell me he's a terrible bore.'
Second Man: 'I've got to go. I'm Cavan O'Connor.'

*   *   *

A young Irish army cadet was attending a selection board.
'Well,' said a ribbon-bedecked general, 'what must an officer be before he can have a funeral with full military honours?'
'Dead,' answered the bright lad.

*   *   *

Did you hear that Michael O'Hare has been voted the kindest farmer in Ireland? When he plants potatoes he puts them in plastic bags to keep the dirt out of their eyes.

*   *   *

In a Belfast Court it was disclosed that the arresting uniform police officer was really a plainclothes-man in disguise.

*   *   *

'Well what did the doctor say?' asked Paddy's wife as he gently lowered himself into a chair.
'He says I've got to take things easy as I'm suffering from syncopation,' replied Paddy.
'Poor darlin',' said his wife, 'but shure and I'll look after you.'
Not quite sure what her husband's illness was, she consulted a dictionary to find that: Syncopation. An uneven movement from bar to bar.

* * *

A Scotsman came to Ireland for a holiday. He went into a pub on the Falls Road (Catholic quarter) and ordered a drink. Another customer nudged him and asked, 'You a stranger here?' The Scot nodded. 'Are you a Catholic or a Protestant?' he was asked. The Scotsman replied he was a Protestant and was immediately beaten up and had to be taken to hospital. After treatment he came out of hospital and wandered down the Shankill Road (Protestant quarter). He decided he could do with a drink and entered a pub. Again he was asked, Catholic or Protestant. Having received one hammering he played safe and said 'Catholic'. Again he got a hammering and had to be taken to hospital. After leaving hospital he flew back to Scotland. He met a friend who said 'I thought you were in Ireland on holiday.'
'Don't mention that place to me. Man, it's a terrible country . They're all heathens over there. If you follow the Lord at all they give you a hammering.'

* * *

A priest, his face red from wind and rain, approached a policeman in Dublin. He huddled into his upturned collar.

Priest: 'Can you tell me the time, please?'

Policeman: 'They'll be open in ten minutes.'

*   *   *

Two young Irishmen in a Canadian regiment were going into the trenches for the first time, and their captain promised them fifty pence for every German they killed. Pat lay down to rest, while Mick performed the duty of watching. Pat had not lain long when he was awakened by Mick shouting: 'They're comin''.

'Who's comin'?' shouts Pat.

'The Germans,' replies Mick.

'How many are there?'

'About fifty thousand.'

'Begorrah,' shouts Pat, jumping up and grabbing his rifle, 'our fortune's made.'

*   *   *

'Well,' said the prospective father-in-law, 'you'll have no objection to a drink.'

'Begorrah,' replied Paddy, 'up to now I've never had one.'

'Bejabbers! Never had a drink?'

'No, an objection.'

*   *   *

40

Paddy: Bridget darling, if rosy cheeks are a sign of good health then you're considerably fitter on one side of your face than the other.

* * *

Danny: 'By just looking into a girl's eyes I can tell what she's thinking.'
Paddy: 'It must be very discouraging.'

* * *

Irish Sergeant: 'Now then, you lot, what have you been doing?'
Pvt. Murphy: 'I've been settin' fuses.'
Pvt. Kelly: 'I've been settin' the saw.'
Pvt. O'Kane: 'I've been settin' the fire.'
Pvt. Flynn: 'I've been settin' still.'

* * *

Irish wife at bedside of sick husband.
Irish Wife: 'Is there no hope, doctor?'
Irish Doctor: 'I don't know. What are you hoping for?'

* * *

Priest at christening and forgetting the date.
Priest: 'Let me see, Bridget, it's the 22nd, isn't it?'
Bridget: 'No, Father, it's only the third. Two boys and a girl.'

* * *

Priest: 'You won't sin anymore, Shaun?'
Shaun: 'Indeed I won't, Father.'
Priest: 'And you'll attend Mass every Sunday?'
Shaun: 'Indeed I will, Father.'
Priest: 'And you'll go to confession every month?'
Shaun: 'Indeed I will, Father.'
Priest: 'And you'll pay all your debts?'
Shaun: 'Now just a minute, Father. You're not talking anymore, you're talking business.'

* * *

'Why won't you marry me?' demanded Paddy. 'There isn't anyone else is there?'
'Oh, Paddy,' sighed Biddy, 'there must be.'

* * *

Errol Flynn, the Hollywood-made Irishman, was once asked when he first began to like girls.
'The minute I discovered they weren't boys,' wagged the grinning Flynn.

* * *

The following appeared in an Irish newspaper under situation vacant. 'Wanted sausage maker. State religion.'

* * *

O'Reilly wandered backstage between the acts of a musical revue and innocently started to enter a room clearly marked 'CHORUS GIRLS' DRESSING ROOM. POSITIVELY NO ADMITTANCE.'
A watchman caught him by the arm. 'Can't you read?' he hollered pointing at the sign.
'Who's smoking?' demanded O'Reilly.

*   *   *

Foreman: 'Hurry and tell Paddy that trench must be shored – it's dangerous.'
Mick: He knows. We're just digging him out.'

*   *   *

Mick: 'What are you going to do for a living.'
Paddy: 'Write.'
Mick: 'Write what?'
Paddy: 'Home.'

*   *   *

Farmer O'Neill had been invited to supper by his neighbour Farmer Kelly. Expecting that his homeward journey would be dark, he had taken a stable lamp. The drink was not spared and the men sat long over their glasses.

O'Neill, however, reached home in safety guided by his lamp.

Next morning he received the following note from his friend:

'O'Neill, I am returning your stable lamp with bearer. Please send back my parrot and cage.'

*   *   *

'Strategy,' answered Private Murphy to a selection board, 'is when you don't let the enemy discover dat you're out of ammunition by keeping on firing.'

*   *   *

Bridget: 'I've broken my glasses. Will I have to be examined all over again.'

Dr O'Kane: 'No, Bridget, just your eyes.'

*   *   *

Doctor: 'You mustn't have excitement of any kind.'

Paddy: 'What? Can't I even look at them in the street?'

*   *   *

NEWS ITEM

An Irishman was admitted to hospital with severe burns after ducking for chips at a Halloween party.

*   *   *

. . . and in Belfast last night two buildings were severely damaged by fire and arson was suspected. Later, the police arrested Fred Arson and charged him with the offences. . . .

* * *

Sign in an Irish barber's shop.
DON'T WORRY IF YOUR HAIR FALLS OUT. SUPPOSE IT ACHED AND HAD TO BE PULLED LIKE TEETH!

* * *

Young Paddy: 'My sister's getting married next week and she's upstairs getting her torso ready.'

* * *

Bridget: 'My boyfriend gave me an empty watch case last night.'
Teresa: 'An empty watch case?'
Bridget: 'Yes, he's giving me the works tonight.'

* * *

Customer: 'I came in to get something for my wife.'
Irishman Salesman: 'What are you asking for her?'

* * *

Mike: 'I was hypnotized once.'
Pat: 'I'm a married man too.'

* * *

45

An Irish builder, when returning thanks to those who drank his health, modestly observed that he was 'more fitted for the scaffold than for the platform.'

* * *

You can't kiss an Irish girl unexpectedly. Only sooner than she thought you would.

* * *

Clancy: 'Are you going to Murphy's wedding?'
Flynn: 'No wedding for me. My fighting days are over.'

* * *

'Ah,' said the pipe-smoking Irishman in a reflective mood. 'There's one compensation in being a woman. You don't have to marry one.'

* * *

One Belfast producer decided to be sure of his new stage show by having nineteen costumes for the twenty dancing girls.

* * *

Heard at a Dublin Hospital.
'Any scars on you?'
'Don't smoke them, have a cigarette.'

* * *

Rory O'Rourke, the Irish poet, has just published his latest work; it goes like this:

Ickety tickety tock
    Two mice ran up her sock
One reached her garter –
    The other was smarter
Ickety tickety tock!

*   *   *

Irish Drunk: 'Shay, officer, where am I?'
Policeman: 'Piccadilly, corner of Haymarket.'
Irish Drunk: 'Never mind the street, just tell me the town.'

*   *   *

Two lawyers standing before an Irish judge got into a fierce argument.
At last one lawyer lost his temper and shouted at his opponent.
'Sir, you are the biggest fool that I have had the misfortune to set eyes on.'
'Order, order,' said the Irish judge gravely. 'You seem to forget that I am in the room.'

*   *   *

First Irish Businessman:
'How's business?'
Second Irish Businessman:
'Kindly remove your hat when you speak of it.'

*   *   *

In Ireland marriage is not a word – it is a sentence.

*   *   *

A Bishop visiting his diocese asked the children in school if they could explain the Sacrament of Holy Matrimony.
Up jumped little Patrick Murphy. 'It's a period of suffering and torment man has to go through to prepare for a higher life.'
'You stupid boy,' said the Parish Priest, 'that will be Purgatory you're describing.'
'Never mind, Father,' said the Bishop. 'We cannot tell, the boy may be right.'

*   *   *

A number of prisoners escaped from a top-security prison in Ireland today by using a helicopter. The police have set up road blocks throughout the province.

*   *   *

An Irishman was arrested today when he made an obscene telephone call and reversed the charge.

*   *   *

Waiter: 'I have stewed kidney, boiled tongue, fried liver, pig's feet.'
Irish Diner: 'Don't tell me your troubles, just get me something to eat.'

*   *   *

Foreman: 'You don't know what good honest work is.'
Paddy: 'No. What good is it?'

* * *

Englishman: 'And is this your most charming wife?'
Irishman: 'No, it's the only one I've got.'

* * *

The manager of an English touring company tele-
gramed to the proprietor of a theatre in County Down
where his company was to appear:
'Would like to hold rehearsal at your theatre tomorrow at three o'clock. Have your stage-manager,
stage-carpenter, property-man, chief electrician and
all stage hands present at that hour.'
Four hours later he received this reply:
'All right. He will be there.'

* * *

Scene at a Dublin Court.
Judge: 'Are you charged with murder?'
Mike: 'No, sor.'
Judge: 'I'm glad of that, there's an awful lot of murder
around. Are you charged with stealing?'
Mike: 'No, sor.'
Judge: 'I'm glad of that, there's an awful lot of stealing
around. Are you charged with arson?'
Mike: 'No, sor, and I'm bet you're glad of that too.'

* * *

LORNE

Joe Kelly was telling his friend about the terrib[le]
he had with a policeman.
'It was terrible. The copper kept hitting me with his
baton and I kept hitting him with empty bottles.'
His friend looked interested and asked: 'Who won?'
'He did. I couldn't empty the bottles quickly enough.'

*　　*　　*

Paddy says he wishes girls wouldn't wear very tight
jeans as it affects his breathing.

*　　*　　*

NEWS ITEM
Mick King of Dublin who won The Irish Milking
Championship says he didn't do it alone as he owes
his success to udders.

*　　*　　*

Irish Son: 'What part of speech is woman, da?'
Irish Da: 'She's the whole of it, son.'

*　　*　　*

First Irishman: 'Does he stutter all the time?'
Second Irishman: 'No, only when he talks.'

*　　*　　*

51

An Ulster Orangeman and his wife were having a holiday in London and wished to go to a stage show. Passing a theatre they noticed the play running there was 'Twelfth Night'.

They decided it would be good and got a couple of seats.

After the play had proceeded for half-an-hour the Ulsterman's patience gave out and he snorted: 'Come away out of this, Mary, I'm fed up. "Twelfth Night" and they haven't even a drum!'

*　　*　　*

When grandma tipped her seat over and fell on her face in the kitchen after sneaking a jar of Mahoney's home-made Irish whiskey, he called upstairs to his wife, 'Belle, you better come down – your old lady's gone off her rocker.'

*　　*　　*

We heard today that Ballymora has been officially declared a foot in mouth area.

*　　*　　*

Immediately after the ceremony in the Register Office, O'Keefe dashed across to the Prudential to take out some maritime insurance.

*　　*　　*

When the firm said they were going to make McConey redundant he asked if that meant he would be given an assistant.

*   *   *

Eamonn O'Toole is now in the Royal Navy. Originally he wanted to work in the N.A.A.F.I. but his spelling let him down.

*   *   *

You can easily spot an Irish butcher. There's more blood on him than on the meat.

*   *   *

An Irish detective who found a corpse in the living-room was so confused he had to be taken home in an ambulance.

*   *   *

Neil went all over the county trying to find a hosier who could sell him three matching socks because he had entered the three-legged race at the county fair.

*   *   *

We heard a haunting melody coming from the ball-room. It was haunting because the Irish 5-piece band were murdering it.

*   *   *

An Irishman in Monte Carlo on holiday went into a casino and a smart-looking attendant asked, 'Do you wish some chips, m'sieur,' and Mike said, 'Yes, if you would, and a fillet of haddock if you have it.'

*　　*　　*

One Irish hero recalls that one of his ancient ancestors was such a rogue and villain that the authorities hanged him four times.

*　　*　　*

One Irishman freely admits that stupidity can be hereditary because he remembers his mother telling him he was a chip off the old blockhead.

*　　*　　*

One night Sean stayed up late and happened to hear the radio state that the B.B.C. was closing down, so in the morning he rang Broadcasting House to ask when the sale would begin.

*　　*　　*

An Irish shrimper always used to use his thumb and index finger to demonstrate the size of any catch that got away.

*　　*　　*

Three disconcerted Irishmen wanted to find a simple way of committing suicide with one single bullet so they put their heads together.

*   *   *

Paddy was acting as route director in a car rally and he seemed to be having trouble. The driver sneaked a look to find out the problem and found his pilot trying to fold up a globe.

*   *   *

They have special Irish midgets at Clancy's Evergreen Bar to serve English visitors who drink themselves under the tables.

*   *   *

An Irishman struck his wife several times in anger because she came out with a dirty word. Work.

*   *   *

When Irish taxidermists have a holiday you'll find most of them in Stankey's Stew Parlour, stuffing themselves.

*   *   *

It was a cold winter night in Mullagh and McClusky berated his wife because she kept throwing log after log on the fire to keep warm. Says McClusky, 'The way you's piling on the fuel anyone would tink dose tings grow on trees!'

*　　*　　*

Peggy O'Neil went and bought one of those mod bras with skimpy straps and open cups, just because the lingerie shop had them marked '50% Off'. And that's how she wore it.

*　　*　　*

The McManuses had a boarding house near the coast where English visitors were most welcome. It was only a stone's throw from the sea . . . and all the windows were broken.

*　　*　　*

'Shure,' he said, 'this is one of them rare Irish Summer days when I sit and wish I was alive.'

*　　*　　*

An Irish migrant to Down Under wanted to try surf riding on Bondi Beach but his horse refused to go near the water.

*　　*　　*

After suffering the pangs of poverty to an extent that disaster stared him in the face, O'Reilly took the coward's way out. He got a job.

*   *   *

They sent McKeady to prison for something that he didn't do. He didn't jump into the getaway Jag fast enough.

*   *   *

Then there's that heroic Irishman who won a marine medal for bravery beyond the call of duty. He rescued a girl from a lifeguard who had rescued her from his best friend.

*   *   *

Alcohol is said to be a colourless mobile fluid with a high refraction index and possesses a faint smell and has a slight acid burning taste that diminishes in dilution with water; it inhibits freezing and the formula is approximately C_2H_6O. Despite all that, Smiley O'Toole is sticking with it until they invent something *better*.

*   *   *

When he went on holiday, another Irishman friend said, 'Drop me a line,' so while he was fishing off the bank near the holiday hotel he baited a second rod for his friend.

*   *   *

57

He wanted to commit suicide by throwing himself under a car but the salesman at the Rover showroom chased him away.

* * *

The National Irish Jazz Band were asked to play something typically ethnic so when they found out what it was they challenged Scotland at Tossing the Pickaxe.

* * *

An Irishman decided to blow himself up, but he couldn't find a pump powerful enough.

* * *

An Irishman was stupid enough to wear a stiff starched collar when he went to Wimbledon Finals, and his head fell off.

* * *

How does an Irishman make love? He hires a stand-in.

* * *

A tourist went into a Dublin eating house and asked, 'Is the fish fresh?' and the waiter said, 'Wait till I've grabbed the little B— and I'll tell you.'

* * *

O'Hara entered the Talent Contest and the number he elected to sing was 'I Could Have Dunced All Night'.

*   *   *

Paddy on phone to doctor: 'Me phoor wife has gone an' dislocated her jawbone and she's in such agony I wonder would yez be able to come along in a day or two, sor?'

*   *   *

'I'm going to the art gallery,' said Shamus, 'to have a head made of my wife's bust.'

*   *   *

Terms indicated in Irish policy:
'The total sum will be paid to you in one single figure at the time of death, and must be applied for by post unless you wish to collect it yourself.'

*   *   *

Irish local wedding notice:
'The couple looked very happy. The bride's going-away outfit was a pale blue gabardine suit with matching coat. Both are very well known locally.'

*   *   *

Notice: 'The Irish Wildlife Association is concerned about the nudist colony based near Baillkilgoy Bridge and the executive officers intend to have a closer look at it.'

* * *

An Irish doctor treated a patient in a novel manner yesterday by using the power of hypnosis to enable her to have a baby without discomfort. The experiment was a tremendous achievement in medical terms because the lady in question wasn't pregnant.

* * *

Statistics indicate that during a normal day's work a conductor will walk as much as 33 miles. His Irish driver can't understand why he doesn't take a bus.

* * *

Mary O'Hara became disenchanted with being a barrister so she dropped her briefs and started soliciting.

* * *

An Irish physicist has discovered that the difference between a singer and a go-go girl is that the singer only has one bobbin.

* * *

How to recognize an Irish bath. The taps are fixed to the outside and the shower unit is fed through the waste pipe.

*　　*　　*

At the cricket match Clancy scored three runs and the lady who suffered the damage to her stockings clouted him with her parasol.

*　　*　　*

An Irishman has been given the job of organizing Enoch Powell's world tour. It starts with a State Visit to Trinidad.

*　　*　　*

Clancy joined the A.A. and when he requested a route to the north of Scotland they directed him through Gloucester via Swansea, over the Conway Bridge through Dartmouth tunnel and through Spaghetti Junction, to Rhyl. Later he realized he had the wrong A.A.

*　　*　　*

Callahan had to go to the dentist. He sat down and asked the dentist if he could have chloroform. 'Don't be stupid, it's just a simple little adjustment to your dental plate,' he was told. Callahan said, 'I don't care. I just can't stand staring into your ugly face.'

*　　*　　*

An Irishman decided to make himself a good strong fishing net and he ended up with a net two miles long and forty yards wide because his wife wouldn't show him how to cast off.

*   *   *

O'Keefe was in a very parlous state of exhaustion. He went to the doctor who gave him a large bottle of tonic, but the poor patient couldn't get up enough steam to pull the cork out.

*   *   *

Paddy has finally given up smoking. He got fed up when he realized he was using three matches every time he wanted to get a flame from his cigarette lighter.

*   *   *

'Coalface' O'Hagan always sneaked into the cinema for half price on the basis that he was a miner.

*   *   *

O'Connor sat and consumed two full bottles of 'Ireland's Own' pure malt whiskey in the evening. He wasn't really thirsty but he was in a hurry to make a matching pair of reading lamps.

*   *   *

When Shaun was three years old his parents took him away from Killbery village because work prospects were hopeless.

*   *   *

He painted his sundial with bright white paint so that he could see the time in a fog.

*   *   *

This Irishman was in Spain and kept bragging he could lick the bull. Anyway, the bull tossed him for it and the Irishman came down heads.

*   *   *

It took one Irishman thirty-six years to realize that his literary efforts were extremely mediocre, but by that time he was far too rich and famous a novelist to bother about it anymore.

*   *   *

'Are you Mick Pleranky?'
'Yes, sor.'
'Very well. Take the stand.'
'I will that, your honour.'
'No, no, you old fool. Bring it back!'

*   *   *

Alcoholic Calhoun dashed out of his house brandishing two king-size tankards.
'What's the panic?' shouted another Irishman across the street.
Calhoun said, 'Hurry and get a bucket, the radio says there's a big storm brewing.'

*   *   *

Their truck was gradually sliding down the hill and the little Irish man couldn't hold it back. He yelled at the big Irish porter who was his assistant. 'Fer Pete's sake, put some chocks under the front wheels.'
'That's no good,' said the other, 'I've only got Maltesers and they's be too soft.'

*   *   *

Pat: 'It's freezing. I'm chilled to the bone.'
Clancy: 'Well, why don't you put your hat on?'

*   *   *

'Have you got a cigarette, Neil?'
'Yes, thanks. Loads of them.'

*   *   *

Mallory joined a tough razor gang in Gorteen but it wasn't very successful because he could never get close enough to a plug socket when the action started.

*   *   *

Calhoun has invented a watch that is guaranteed to last a whole lifetime. If the mainspring should break it automatically slashes your wrist.

*   *   *

Always an opportunist, Clancy walked all the way to the heart of Australia because he'd heard it was virgin territory.

*   *   *

The Irishman was very distressed and crying his eyes out so his wife said, 'It's no good crying over spilt milk, Shamus.' He stopped crying and said, 'Begorrah, I taut it was whiskey!'

*   *   *

An Irish father studied his three daughters and remarked to his wife, 'Have yez ever considered those there girls of ours? Cara is thin and Everleen is thin but our poor Kathleen is thinner than the other two put together!'

*   *   *

There is a notorious juvenile detention centre near Paddiwaddy where the authorities have had to bar all the windows to prevent people breaking in.

*   *   *

There's a new hospital in Belfast where the nurses wake patients up twice a day to give them their sleeping pills.

*   *   *

An hotel owner in Ballycorny has just opened another hotel, offering cheaper rates to visitors prepared to share the bathroom. Which is across town.

*   *   *

Maureen worked at the Nudist Sun Camp Casino, and she gave in her notice last night because in a few months' time there's to be a wedding and she wants to be married in white.

*   *   *

The latest idea in Irish hotels is television in every bedroom. But the chap who installed the sets made them relay instead of play-back.

*   *   *

How can you recognize an Irish psychoanalyst? It's that Mick walking down the avenue with a couch on his head.

*   *   *

Paddy thinks that blue serge is an increase in hot movies.

*   *   *

When Paddy was told by his boss to take the piano up two flights, he phoned the airport and reserved tickets.

*   *   *

Paddy was having dinner in an exclusive casino with his boss, and he kept kicking at the carpet and peering under the table. His boss said, 'Why are you fidgeting about?'
Paddy said, 'I want to see the floor show.'

*   *   *

Paddy was on a visit to London's backwaters from Ballymenny and as he passed a dilapidated block of flats a skinny woman fell from a window and landed in a garbage bin on the corner. Paddy went closer to get a better look and said, 'Bejabers, back home that one would have been good for another two years yet.'

*   *   *

A pretty Irish girl always hitches her caravan to the car when a man takes her for a ride. That way she doesn't have very far to walk home.

*   *   *

An Irish detective from 13th Division came across a dead body in the living-room of an empty house, so he dragged it into the drawing-room and drew the curtains. When the superintendent arrived he studied the drawing of the curtains and complimented the detective on his artistic ability.

*   *   *

He stayed in an hotel in Rome one night. Very exclusive place it was. At around half-past eleven he rang down for room service . . . they sent up a Jesuit priest and four choirboys.

* * *

O'Toole took his mother-in-law to India for a holiday. She made an absolute pig of herself, especially with curries. The way she ate, it's no wonder the week after they got home there was a famine alert from Delhi to Calcutta. The Indian commissioner would have complained, but he said that in India people like O'Toole's mother-in-law were considered sacred.

* * *

A BBC documentary team were filming a nature programme in Essex. The director asked O'Leary to direct him to the bird sanctuary and O'Leary drew him a route map to the local YWCA.

* * *

I was on this ferry boat watching the waves, with an Irishman on the left of the rail and a young woman on my right. The girl's hat blew off in the wind and when she tried to grab it, she fell overboard. There was quite a swell and she began to panic and shouted up, 'For God's sake, drop me a line!' The Irishman shouted back: 'What's the address?'

* * *

'How many strokes have I taken, Paddy?' asked the golfer.

'I don't know, sor.'

'Call yourself a caddie and you can't count,' said the golfer.

'It's not a caddie you need, sor, it's a calculator.'

* * *

Last season I worked in a summer show at a small Irish seaside resort and it was the worst show they'd ever had on the end of the pier. I know it was the end of the pier because a visitor dynamited it.

* * *

A watchmaker in Belfast went into hospital for an operation but he was so tense he had to wait awhile before the surgeon could get to work. It took him eight days to unwind.

* * *

'You're the biggest scoundrel I ever had the misfortune to employ in me coalyard. I can't teach ye a ting.'

'Well,' said Kelly, 'I sure larnt wun ting since I worked for youse tru the winter.'

'Yes, and what's that?'

'Just that sixteen hundred-weight's a level tun.'

The coal merchant said, 'I change me mind, Kelly, there's hope fer yez, I'm a-thinkin'.'

* * *

Callagan said, 'I went all over the East and when I was in Singapore I even had a ride in a ricochet.' O'Connor scoffed, 'You mean a rickshaw, you old fool.'

Callaghan said, 'Fool yourself. I was coming back.'

* * *

'Oi've a swine of a toothache, me mouth's fair throbbing with the agony of it all. Do you know a good dentist, O'Mara?'

'No, no, you don't need a dentist. I had a terrible toothache meself yesterday but my wife put her arms round me and kissed and cuddled me, and loved me up, and in no time at all the pain went away. You might try the same ting.'

'Well, what do you know! I never reckoned you such a friend . . . Where will I be finding your kindly wife, den?'

* * *

McClusky had twelve bonny children and it was difficult to read a paper. One evening, while his wife was lying down, the front doorbell rang noisily. He opened up and on the threshold stood a tall, imposing, very handsome man gripping a businesslike bag.

'Begorrah!' ejaculated McClusky, 'Come on in then, and Holy Mother of mercy may you be just the piano tuner.'

* * *

A specimen list of answers provided in Irish examination results.

- Electricity was invented by Voltaire in 250 DC.
- Robinson Crusoe was a popular tenor, so called because that was his usual fee for a week's engagement.
- A Norwegian fjord is an automobile with skis in place of wheels.
- Mata Hari was a rambling rose of wildwoods, and part-time spy.
- Karl Marx was the 5th Brother of Chico, Groucho and others.
- Crepe Suzette is what thin paper dresses are made, of.
- A concubine is an amalgamation of several big firms.
- Myxomatosis is when you wipe out mice and rabbis.
- Columbine invented America in a date I have since forgotten.
- A monsoon is a tiny Frenchman.
- Kosher is when your bacon is treated for Hebrew gourmets.
- A psalmist is a person who has red hands.
- A polygon is a decomposed carrot (or possibly, parrot).

*　　*　　*

'O'Connor has become quite adept with his pen.'
'Is he writing another novel?'
'No, but he's reared over twenty-seven pigs.'

*　　*　　*

Reserve soldiers were on manoeuvres on a dark and wet day on the boggy marshland as part of the Irish regiment's training. After six hours of it Clancy decided to pack it in so he sent a signal: 'Wish to desert to the enemy. Radio enemy position. Am soaked to skin, send umbrella.'

They radioed back, 'All units retreated two hours ago and enemy unit wiped out. You better commit suicide to avoid being on a charge.'

*　　*　　*

MORE IRISH ARMY REPORTS

If you are caught in a nuclear attack dig a hole eight feet with your hat and lie in the trench with any others you can find for company and pull grass, pebbles, tin-cans, rubble, etc. over you. This will not help in protecting you, but it does make the place look tidier. Signed, Post Mortem, Sergt. Mike O'Rourke, Reserves.

*　　*　　*

The Irish politician began his speech: 'There is something I want to get off my chest today that has been hanging over my head for weeks, and I'll be glad to put it behind me before we come to the end.'

*　　*　　*

One of our typists, Dora, made a mistake in the office today and the boss made her stay over and do it all again.

*　　*　　*

74

O'Donougue bought himself fifty-seven acres of building land. Then he found he couldn't get it on his truck.

*   *   *

Two Irish visitors were sitting on the beach at Bournemouth, throwing shells at each other . . . 28-pounders.

*   *   *

The Bishop was annoyed and told the Vicar: 'Why did you fill Lord Marner's head with all that stuff about reincarnation?' 'Well,' said the Vicar, 'He's ninety years old so I thought a little talk about resurrections and reincarnation would cheer him up.' The Bishop said: 'You dolt, he was going to leave us £300,000 in his will, and now he's gone and left it to himself.'

*   *   *

An Irish chap visiting the zoo saw a small child being attacked by an escaped baby chimpanzee. He grabbed the nearest weapon, which happened to be a white stick belonging to a blind news-vendor, and with it he beat off the chimp and grasped the child. The next morning English newspapers bore the headline, 'Irishman Trips Beggar and Slays Child's Pet with Stolen Cudgel'.

*   *   *

An illegal immigrant Paki thought he could fiddle nationalization if he became an Irishman, so he visited a brain surgeon who told him that he would need to have three-quarters of his brain removed to become an Irishman.

The Paki said, 'Very good idea. I pay. You fix me up.' However by mistake the doctor removed five-sixths of Paddy's brain and when he woke up he grabbed the surgeon by the lapels and complained: 'Begorrah, old man, you've changed me into an Englishman.'

* * *

O'Connor was summoned for killing a dog. The magistrate asked him how he had missed seeing the dog in the headlights while he was clearly visible with his leg cocked against a tree. O'Connor said: 'I did so see that, your honour, sir, but at the time I thought he was just signalling to turn right.'

* * *

McClusky went into a London pub with a small piglet under his arm. The barman said, 'Where the divil did ye get that scrawny little swine?'

The pig said, 'I won him at Bingo.'

* * *

An Irish inventor has designed a device like a 100-mile long telescope which bends at the thick end so that he can study the ground forty miles away.

* * *

There's a beautiful Irish cabaret artiste working in London as a strip-teaser, wearing hardly any clothes, but screened by a dozen lovely white pigeons. The act closes on Saturday because the birds refuse to take off any more feathers.

* * *

Selena has just bought something for her little Irish bottom drawer. A cure for dry-rot.

* * *

He wants to work as a candid cameraman, so Shamus is looking for a discreet little camera with a lens shaped like a keyhole.

* * *

The only thing that isn't taxed in Cloghan Bend is the village constable's brain power.

* * *

The Irish library is nearly empty. But the librarian, Sheila, is well stacked.

* * *

As a typist she was very very slow, mainly because every time the bell tinkled she knocked off for a cup of tea.

* * *

He was reading one of those intense Irish family novels, the kind that you just can't put down. You have to burn it.

*　　*　　*

Quincy O'Flahaty was wounded by a blank this morning. The postman brought his Income Tax schedule.

*　　*　　*

'Sure and you can't have better than greens for perfect vision,' said the Irish greengrocer. 'Did you ever see a rabbit wearing bifocals?'

*　　*　　*

The Irish customer had come in for some gloves and the salesman assured him that the ones he recommended were well made and guaranteed real cowhide. 'May be,' said the customer, 'but just because it says so on the label isn't proof. Anyone can forge a label and stamp "Cowhide" on it.' The salesman said, 'But there's one thing nobody can forge, sir. Have you not noticed that the gloves have four fingers – the perfect number for genuine cowhide?' 'To be sure,' said the customer, 'What a fool Oi am!'

*　　*　　*

Casey complained, 'That there Palais de Dance they built outside the town is crowded to the roof and all up the staircase. It's not to be wondered that peoples don't go there.'

* * *

Sullivan thought he had it made and that with Eveleen in his arms he was living the life of O'Reilly. Then one night O'Reilly came home unexpected . . .

* * *

'What a wreck that car of yours is! Why don't you paint it?'
'I intend to do exactly that, Mike, but I find the pressure of the spray keeps bending the bodywork into folds.'

* * *

'Are you never going to give up the booze, Malley?'
'Not at all. But I'm considering having me knees soled and heeled to give me a little more comfort in me old age.'

* * *

So this lovely young Irish maid confessed to a little white lie. She told her husband he wasn't really the father of their six lovely children.

* * *

His wife was moaning again so Pat tried to cheer her up. 'Count your blessings,' says he, 'We've got a nice room to live in, and five beautiful kiddies, and all this valuable antique furniture . . .'

'We don't have any antique furniture,' she said, 'not a piece at all.'

Pat said, 'Well we *will* have by the time this lot's paid for.'

*　　*　　*

The Irishman who suffered in the cold weather went to the Scotch Hosiery shop to order a large, chunky warm pullover to be knitted. 'Do you want a deep collar?' the saleslady asked. 'I do, I do, indade I do, and if you can manage it I'll have one of dose lunatic fringes on the bottom.'

*　　*　　*

'Bridie, I'm a fool, I've left my teeth at home.'

'Don't be daft, Eamonn, you have all your *own* teeth.'

'Dat's what I said, me darlin', I'm not coming to your Mam's.'

*　　*　　*

Paddy was returning from the cemetery after attending the burial of his wife.

As he was approaching his front door a tile fell off the roof and hit him on the head.

Looking to the sky in surprise, he muttered: 'Begorrah! Are you there already?'

*　　*　　*

LORNE

Casey surprised his wife with a thick beaver fur coat last night . . . She'd never seen him in one before.

*   *   *

'Sure an' I'd like a ticket to Kennon beach.'
'Are yez First Class or Third Class, O'Malley?'
'You know full well, Clancy, I'm upper middle class.'

*   *   *

The Irishman inserted a notice in the *Belfast Gazette*: 'To Moira and Keith Regan two foine male and one female births. Others please copy.'

*   *   *

'Oi wuz sent to prison for something I didn't do!'
'Bad cess to the magistrate that served you such a wrong, Sullivan, and what are you doing about it? Sue de court?'
'I think not. I didn't pay the missus's affiliation order.'

*   *   *

An Irishman was on the tram with his mate Terry and right opposite was a lovely colleen whom he wanted to impress. So he said in a loud voice to Terry, 'You realize that I'm not really as tall as this, I happen to be sitting on me wallet.'

*   *   *

The minister was exhorting his flock to behave. 'Flee from the wrath to come. Do no evil. I warn the transgressor that when judgement day comes there will be a weeping and a wailing and a great gnashing of teeth.'
Darrel O'Leary stood up and complained, 'Den I shall be left out, on account I don't have no teeth!'
The minister roared, 'Teeth will be provided.'

* * *

On the tram when the lady conductress came to Paddy he tendered a £1 note and said, 'My Fare, Lady.'
She kicked him hard on the knee, pulled him up by the shoulder, pushed him and said, 'Hop-Along, Cassidy!'

* * *

Paddy bought something for his sister's bottom drawer . . . a kneeling pad.

* * *

An Irish Martian felt weak and consulted the local doctor, who gave him a tonic for metal fatigue.

* * *

Clancy visited the doctor's surgery and the medic looked at his running eyes and fevered brow and said scientifically, 'Clancy, I bet you have 'flu!'
Clancy said, 'Not at all. I walked. You'd never get me up in one of them things.'

* * *

Murphy said, 'See here, slob, you haven't fooled me. I saw you through our curtains, making love to my wife last night, and I clobbered her good and hard, so there.' The other man said, 'No, you didn't see me, Murph, because I was over at the site all night, for overtime.' Murphy said, 'Begorrah, I hit the poor creature for nothing.'

*   *   *

This Irishman found the home number of the guy who owned a gigantic store in Dublin, and he rang his home and asked, 'What time does your store open?'
It was three o'clock in the morning and the store boss was annoyed and rang off. Ten minutes later the caller rang again, asking the store owner, 'What time does your store open?' The boss snapped, 'Look, it's the middle of the night. Why don't you go along about nine in the morning and then they'll let you in.'
The caller said, 'I don't want to get in, I want to be let out. I'm here now.'

*   *   *

They were in church when Riley, the vicar, announced that an immediate plate collection would take place to raise funds to repair the holy candlesticks. On hearing the announcement Rory O'Connor fell in a dead faint and his two brothers carried him out into the fresh air.

*   *   *

When the Channel Tunnel idea was brought up for the umpteenth time, an Irish contractor contacted the authorities with an original suggestion. He wanted to have one gang start working from the French side and another gang tunnelling from the Dover end. All good, reliable, hard-working Irish experts. The Tunnel authorities asked the contractor, 'Why is your proposition better then the old original plan?' He replied, 'If you do it my way you'll get two tunnels for the price of one.'

*   *   *

Irish crooks always commit their crimes in the months of November to April because if they are sentenced in that period they are sure to miss a lot of double summer-time work in prison.

*   *   *

Shayne crossed a tom-cat with an octopus because he wanted a clutch of eight kittens.

*   *   *

A lively young Irish lady from Wexford pulled into a garage with engine trouble and asked for help. The garage attendant gave the car a quick check and told her that she had a short circuit in the ignition and she said, 'How long will it take you to stretch it?'

*   *   *

A newly married woman tried to get an immediate divorce on the grounds that she was getting torn to death in bed every night. Her husband insisted on wearing six army medals on his pyjama pocket. And he wasn't even *in* the Irish Dragoons – he bought them in a second-hand shop.

*　　*　　*

The motorist broke down on a deserted stretch of road about a million miles from home. Luckily a farm cart trundled along an hour later and the driver shouted to the Irish agriculturer, 'Hey, can you lend a hand?' The drover nodded and said, 'Sorry, sor, me hands is fixed to me wrists but I has a wooden leg you can borrow if it'll help.'

*　　*　　*

McManus went back to the radio shop to return a transistor radio. He complained that he did not know he would need to keep buying new batteries every week. The salesman said they could not take it back as it was scratched. 'It says there on the poster "Money Back If Not Satisfied",' McManus reminded the salesman. The salesman said, 'But we *are* quite satisfied with the money so we don't have to return it.' McManus said, 'You needn't bother anyway because I nicked it in the first place.'

*　　*　　*

Fergus was an avid reader. He read so many books that it became difficult to find anything new. Finally he had a brainwave, went to the local W. H. Smith store and asked, 'Got any good Easterns?'

*　　*　　*

'Did you have a good time on your visit to Moscow, Pat?'
'It wasn't too bad. Nice hotel. But the television had me baffled.'
'What sort of programmes were you watching?' asked Mike.
'I wasn't. The TV was watching *me*.'

*　　*　　*

McClusky went to dine in a restaurant in Wexford and ordered the day's menu. When the soup arrived McClusky pointed to his plate in which a large bluebottle was swimming. The waiter shrugged and said, 'You'll have to be going in for it yourself, I can't swim.'

*　　*　　*

Shelagh: 'Regan, I'm finishin' the ironing so will you be doing me a favour and change the baby?'
'Rubbish, woman, there ain't nothin' wrong with the one we've got!'

*　　*　　*

87

If you want to play golf out at old Ballyvoury watch for lady drivers. There are no route signs.

*　　*　　*

She married an Irish sailor because she wanted to have children and rear admirals.

*　　*　　*

'I've never seen so many folk going to church as there were last Monday evening.'
'I'm not surprised, Mahoney, how often do we have such a big fire at St Mary's; the flames were through the roof.'

*　　*　　*

When Shelagh asked McClusky why he had suddenly stopped loving her he explained he had a train to catch.

*　　*　　*

Bernice was a bit passed it and she told the doctor that the pains came on every ten minutes and lasted half an hour.

*　　*　　*

There's an Irishman who breeds race horses that are so slow it takes them all their time to come in last.

*　　*　　*

Clancy bought a ticket in Paris to see 'The Best Leg-Show In France' and all he got for his money was a view of the six-day round-France Cycle Race.

*   *   *

Irish Whiskey, so they say, not only makes a man see double but also makes him act single.

*   *   *

All new Irish cars are being fitted with fabric upholstery instead of leather because it makes it easier for the motor repair mechanics to wipe their hands.

*   *   *

Mike Connor once spent three weeks having a day out on the Isle of Man.

*   *   *

When the Guarda put a price of £15.34 on his head, the missing crook, Kelly, gave himself up and claimed the reward. Then he found out the police had paid off in the same money he had been forging.

*   *   *

The wife of the man in the condemned cell took a long piece of strong cord with her when she visited him. She didn't know for certain whether he had to provide his own.

*   *   *

Anthea entered the International Irish Beauty Contest and she received a very high recommendation. The judges recommended she went home and stayed there.

*   *   *

The Irish Song Contest to find the best piece of music for the forthcoming year has finished. However, before the winning musicians can be rewarded they will have to exhume Tchaikovsky and Strauss for 1st and 2nd places.

*   *   *

Regan has invented a new method of fishing. He only has to sprinkle a pint or two of poteen into the river and the salmon come up ready canned.

*   *   *

The patient Murphy was in the doctor's surgery as tight as a tourniquet and the doctor admonished him severely. 'Murph,' says he, 'there are many better scientific ways to treat double pneumonia than swigging six singles of Irish Scotch.'
Murph said, 'Shure an' all of us knows that; but who cares?'

*   *   *

Bernie O'Toole boasts that he always gets up at the crack of dawn – because he can see the sunrise better.

*   *   *

A pretty Irish colleen volunteered as a blood donor and when they asked her what type she was she said, 'Sultry and very affectionate.'

*   *   *

Sean insists that one of his ancient ancestors was such a dangerous villain he was executed three times.

*   *   *

Mike's sister seems to want to change her religion. Yesterday she went for a little cantor in the woods.

*   *   *

Shamus was determined his son must become a farmer and so he apprenticed him to a pharmacy.

*   *   *

Diana dieted for two weeks and all she lost was a fortnight.

*   *   *

Mike's elderly mother-in-law was visiting her daughter and she took a bath without knowing that Mike had just painted it with very poor enamel which would not dry out. She was stuck fast, so Mike had to write a letter to the manufacturer for advice.

*   *   *

The roof of the chapel was leaking and the priest asked for volunteers to raise funds for its repair.

Mike offered his services.

About a week later the priest met Mike who was staggering from side to side as a result of having imbibed too freely.

Mike was apologetic.

'I'm collecting for the roof, Father,' he said. 'Every one of the neighbours I called on insisted on giving me a wee drop after paying his subscription.'

The priest was shocked. 'Are there no teetotallers in the parish, Mike?'

'Oh yes,' was the reply. 'Shure there's teetotallers. I've written to them.'

* * *

The scene is the Pearly Gate.

St Patrick has taken over from St Peter after a heavenly punch-up.

St Patrick: 'Your name?'

Applicant: 'Sean O'Brien.'

St Patrick: 'Have you gambled, lied, stolen, smoked or taken liquor?'

Applicant: 'Heavens! No!'

St Patrick: 'Have you cheated, stolen, sworn, played a guitar?'

Applicant: 'What do you take me for?'

St Patrick: 'Have you ever been promiscuous?'

Applicant: 'Do you mind!!!'

St Patrick: (*aside to his accountant*) 'What the hell delayed this nut-case?'

* * *

The Irish editor was sent a novel for consideration and it was so awful that he had to rewrite it in order to render it fit to reject.

*　　*　　*

The Irish Keep-Fit Slogan:
Health is a grand thing to be blessed with, especially when you're sick.

*　　*　　*

'I'm fed up, O'Malley. Ever since our honeymoon ended my wife's been hitting the ceiling.'
'Quit moaning, Neil, and be glad she's such a lousy shot.'

*　　*　　*

'Mine was a run-away marriage.'
'How romantic!'
'Romantic, phooey. She caught up with me!'

*　　*　　*

'O'Hara is getting married tomorrow.'
'That's great! I never did loike the auld swine.'

*　　*　　*

An Englishman thinks sitting down. An American thinks pacing the cocktail lounge. A Frenchman thinks in the back of a taxi. The Irishman thinks he's got nothing to think about.

*   *   *

Shane was sitting in his office crying his unsmiling Irish eyes out. Bob Reiss walked in, noticed the state of business failure, and shrugged, 'It's no good crying over spilt milk.'
Shane said, 'I gotta, on account of Moran cut off me Guinness line to the pub below.'

*   *   *

Clusky always takes his family on holiday in November for the summer because it's easier to get deck-chairs then.

*   *   *

Mahoney reported his wife missing so the Guarda came and they asked for a detailed description. It was three in the morning before they stopped laughing.

*   *   *

The doctor gave out the news that Bridgette had been blessed with triplets. Her husband cried in disbelief, 'I demand a recount, doctor, sor; I remember that night and one must be missing.'

*   *   *

'Hey, that you, Clancy? Get yourself over here, we're having a shindig!'

'No can do, Patrick. I've got me a case of gingivitis.'

'Hell, Clancy, fetch it across; these bastards'll drink anything.'

* * *

If there are a dozen cows in a meadow you can usually pick out the Irish bullocks. They'll be the ones standing.

* * *

At a village level crossing close to Kancully Bridge, the gate-keeper always has the bars mid-way open because he's half-expecting an express.

* * *

There is a very determined bigot in County Clone who swears that he would sooner die than be buried in a Protestant graveyard.

* * *

An Irish Memory is what a man forgets with when he owes either money or a favour.

* * *

Flahaty had gone down to the sluice and nearly got himself drowned. They pumped him and pummelled him and gave him the kiss of life but it wasn't too successful. Then O'Hara suggested, 'How about trying a bit of the hard stuff! I've a full bottle in me pocket, I was taking to tonight's feast.'

The man doing the resuscitation growled, 'You idjit, hard liquor could finish him off in his state.' The dying man pulled himself up, grabbed the bottle and snorted, 'You keep outa this, O'Connor, it ain't *your* whiskey!' He then took a reviving draught, coughed twice and expired.

*   *   *

The suffering wife was in the witness box. 'Mrs O'Sullivan, are you telling me that this poor pitiful physical wreck in the courtroom here, who can scarcely stand up, could have given you that black eye and broken two fingernails?' said the judge.

She said, 'He wasn't a physical wreck, your honour; not when he *started* on me.'

*   *   *

Clancy was on one of his rare visits to church. He'd only been sat ten minutes when he nudged his neighbour and said, 'I see that you have a badge of membership for the church of the Christian Scientist.'

'That's right, brother.'

Clancy said, 'Then shift over and change places, I'm sitting in a divil of a draught.'

*   *   *

The *Belfast Daily Gazette* recorded a launching in this manner. 'The Countess banged a bottle of Irish Chianti against her bulbous bow and amid loud applause from the seething crowd she slid majestically on her greasy bottom into the mighty sea . . .'

*　　*　　*

An Irish alibi is partial proof that the accused was in two places at the same time but was delayed, and in any case it was two other chaps.

*　　*　　*

The consensus of opinion is that an Englishman thinks too much and is usually wrong; a Scot thinks twice before he speaks and nobody understands except another Scot; and the Irishman speaks long before he thinks, even though he doesn't know what he's talking about.

*　　*　　*

'Holy smoke!' ejaculated Terry O'Neil, 'the church is on fire!' An Irish bystander inquired, 'What's ejaculated mean?'

*　　*　　*

The Irish have an old monastic Order which maintains the virtue of silence. Three of the hermits had been together for ages. One said, 'Did you see that woman going by, with scarcely any clothes on?' A year later, the second monk said, 'Yes, isn't it disgusting?' And so another year came and went. The third one said, 'Why are you always bickering? Good God, the girl's got three or four children now. Leave her alone!' And the following year the first monk snapped: 'How dare you insinuate! I never touched her!'

*   *   *

An Irish glutton eats so much food you'd think that fruit grows on trees.

*   *   *

Alvin Donoghue took his baby son to the clinic because Maureen was not well and the child needed a nappy change. While he was there a nurse decided to weigh the infant and she told Alvin, 'Good heavens, little Mike weighs scarcely sixteen pounds!' Alvin said, 'Well what do you expect, woman, with me and Bridie only wed three weeks!'

*   *   *

I met an Irishman who was working part-time for Irish Intelligence; he was a full-time half-wit.

*   *   *

Teacher received this letter from the mother of a pupil:
'And don't set our Keith no more sums like how long should it take a man to walk right round the perimeter of Lurgan twice, because his Dad lost two days' work pacing it out, and after going to all that trouble and expense you marked him wrong.'

* * *

Kean asked the local interior decorator to quote for improving the aspect of the house they had bought. Said the expert, O'Mara, 'Wid a couple of coats of enamel on dose walls, dey'll be twice as thick.'

* * *

'Good heavens, Clancy, why on earth are you keeping a moo-cow in your old garden?'
'Well, last week it was 15p, this week it's gone up to 17p a pint, so damn it I'm going to take matters into my own hands.'

* * *

A small boy and a small girl lived close to an Irish nudist resort and whilst they were playing by the fence they saw a knot-hole. The little boy was inquisitive and stood on his tip-toes to look through. His sister asked, 'What are they, Moms or Dadas?' The lad said, 'No way of knowing, they don't have any clothes.'

* * *

The notice in the park said plainly, 'Do not walk on the grass'. So Sean had no alternative than to walk on the flower beds.

*   *   *

It was the day of the Irish Derby. An infrequent race-goer waved to a mounted jockey and said amiably, 'Your horse seems hot and exhausted. I wager he just won the last race.' The jockey said sourly, 'Aw, push off. He got this way walking to the starting-gate.'

*   *   *

The Irish labour contingent arrived on the site and it was immediately visible that all of them had forgotten to bring a spade. The gang boss telephoned his foreman who advised: 'I'll be sending a truck over with the tools, and until it gets there you'll just have to lean on each other.'

*   *   *

The ever-loving Irish Grandma leaned over the side of the cot and croaked, 'Did ye ever see such a broth of a child, oh ye weeny cherub darlin' I could eat ye.' The child turned and said, 'Bejabers! Wid no teeth?'

*   *   *

The bus was crowded when an old Irish woman shuffled on board. A lad tugged her lapel and said, 'Take me seat, grannie.' She said, 'No, tanks, I'm in a hurry. I've no time fer sittin'.'

*   *   *

During retreat at a boys' college in County Mayo the priest who was hearing confessions noticed that each boy concluded by confessing to having thrown rice into the pond. The last boy, however, did not mention this particular matter.
'Haven't you been throwing rice into the pond?' asked the priest.
'Please, Father,' answered the boy, 'I am Rice.'

*   *   *

An Irish gent called on his friend Murphy and found him very worried. 'I've been trying to commit suicide,' said he. His friend suggested, 'Why not put that there rope around your neck and pull it toit?' The other man said, 'Sure, I tried dat and the bloody ting near choked me!'

*   *   *

Incomprehensively, the last coach of the train on a normal route kept getting smashed up by vandals. A porter stationed at Castlebyne came up with an idea. 'Leave the last coach off!'

*   *   *

Shamus O'Toole is looking forward to the show at the Belfast Royal Theatre tonight. Someone told him Black and Decker are appearing in person.

*　　*　　*

A lovely Irish model who used to work on a famous calendar untiringly, thinks she might be back on the job shortly, but one thing bothers her. Does it matter that she missed two months during the spring?

*　　*　　*

They were lying in bed, doing nothing as usual, and Keith said to his wife Clodagh, 'Why the hell do you keep calling me Ivan?'

*　　*　　*

When O'Malley took his brood on holiday to Spain they drank only beer or lemonade. The water was undrinkable without sterilization and O'Malley said sterilization was not permitted in his religion.

*　　*　　*

Sheila got so cold when the nights lengthened that she bought herself eighteen skeins of pink flex and knitted herself an electric blanket.

*　　*　　*

Regan, the ruthless crook, went into a lingerie store and asked the young lady assistant for a pair of tights. She said, 'What size does your wife take?' He said, 'I don't know but it don't matter because I want 'em for me face.'

* * *

O'Mora regrets the passing of the good old times when he worked for the gentry up at the old Lodge. Up until 1966 he had a job French polishing the firewood, but then they went all-electric.

* * *

O'Riley had a greyhound which proved more than a stick-in-the-bog. A colleague advised him: 'Listen, boyo, if you want to do best with that critter, best put a little lead in his ear.'
O'Riley said, 'Sure and how in Hades will I do that?'
'With a rifle, boyo.'

* * *

The Blackpool landlady didn't understand the Irish lad too well but tried her best. At tea she asked him if he would like his eggs on a piece of toast.' He shrugged and said, 'If you don't have any plates, ma'am, I'm sure they'll be just foine, however.'

* * *

'Listen, Una, if we got wed would your dad provide you with a dowry?'
Una nodded and smiled. 'Yes, Fred.'
'And if we wed, would your dad let us live here? Over his pub?'
Una nodded and smiled.
Fred said, 'Will you marry me, then, Una?'
She laughed and said, 'In a pig's eye!'

*　　*　　*

Three muggers set about Sullivan and a fierce battle ensued. Finally the enemy got him down and searched his pockets, collecting 26 pence and a French cent. 'Why the divil did yez make such a fuss about parting with a measley 26 pence?' snorted the ringleader irately.
Sullivan panted, 'Well, sure an' all I tought you wuz after the five-pound note hid in me coat lining.'

*　　*　　*

NOTICE OUTSIDE THE BALLYCONON DISCO:
Gents and Ladies welcome regardless of sex.

*　　*　　*

Mahon won a hundred pounds on the Pools and he invested it wisely in a second-hand piano and a wheel-barrow. The barrow was for taking the piano to the music teacher who lived a mile distant. It was also useful for taking the piano back home after lessons.

*　　*　　*

The lady of the house hired a temporary ╱ while
her sister was away on holiday. One mor.
questioned the girl. 'Clodagh, I find your bra
hanging on the door knob, and your underclot.
under the settee and a neighbour tells me you performed a strip-tease routine for my son! Is it really
true that you entertained my son last night?'
The girl said, 'Well, I did my best, Mam. I did my
best.'

*　　*　　*

Three Irish removal experts were negotiating a heavy
piece of furniture up a steep, bending staircase. It was
a hot sticky day. Suddenly the foreman asked, 'Where
the heck is Callaghan? He was supposed to help us
with this beknighted bloody old wardrobe.' Keith said,
'Aye, so he is, to be sure. He's right here in the
wardrobe keeping the hanging rails in place.'

*　　*　　*

An Irish colleen was snapped on the beach at Killy-
cranky wearing a see-through bra – over her eyes.

*　　*　　*

He sent his girl a bunch by Interflora. He sent
cauliflowers because he approved the wearing of the
green.

*　　*　　*

He went to his panel doctor for a renewal because he noticed that his sexual licence had expired.

* * *

She told her boss that her reason for being late was a severe hangover, so Paddy bought her a larger bra.

* * *

The colleen sent for a man from Rent-a-Gent and when he got there she tore him limb from limb.

* * *

Yesterday Paddy made a real killing in the stock market. He shot his broker.

* * *

Although he's pure Irish he has a lot of hot Spanish blood in his veins. He drinks a whole lot of cheap Costa Brava sherry which he gets free at the docks.

* * *

Patrick was in trouble with his wife when he rolled home at three o'clock in the morning with the excuse that he had been attacked down an alley by two girl muggers who danced in their spare time in a cabaret show.

* * *

Maureen got a job as a stripper at an Irish cabaret club and when it was her turn to appear the audience yelled, 'Get 'em back on, get 'em back on!'

*   *   *

Riley was arrested for gross indecency and his defence was that he had only done it *143* times.

*   *   *

A terrorist died and went to heaven. The Commissar up there said, 'I'm sorry, we don't take hi-jackers.' The applicant shouted, 'Nuts. Tell St Peter he's got just three minutes to get out!'

*   *   *

They were going to arrest Mike for being a dangerous driver but he was sent to a lunatic asylum instead when the chief constable searched him and found a season ticket for Liverpool soccer club.

*   *   *

One Irishman sold a migrant Indian the whole of his garden lawn for £10,000, claiming it was a Paddy field.

*   *   *

The local committee elected Sean the sole judge at the Sheep Dog Trials in Ballymelly, and he gave two of the dogs life imprisonment and a third was fined £100.

*   *   *

Phil O'Brian fell in love and married a check-out girl from Tesco Stores. Because she wasn't a practising Catholic Tescos gave her a cash-register-office wedding.

*   *   *

Last night an entire six-floor building was gutted. The Irish owners say that it will be at least a year before production of their Infallible-Inflammable Fire Extinguishers will be back in production, and the Irish nightwatchman has been suspended. Efforts are being made to cut him down.

*   *   *

As Murphy descended from the airliner in a groggy state of unreality and stupor he proclaimed, 'Tanks for dem last two rides, I had, Mr Pilot.' '*Two*?' asked the hostess. 'The first and de last, me darlin'.'

*   *   *

'When I was in prison my wife baked a cake and hid a saw inside it but when I tried to escape through the bars the saw was too blunt.'
'So you did your full sentence?'
'No, I managed to smash my way out through the stone walls with the cake.'

*   *   *

Then there's Casey that was. He was carrying a load of dynamite across to the factory when the whistle went – and he downed tools enthusiastically, like.

*   *   *

'Look, I hate you so much I wouldn't throw you a rope if you were drowning in a sewer,'
'Don't waste your time, I wouldn't touch your rotten rope in any case.'

*   *   *

There's this Irish colleen who married a barber and gave him all her money to start his own shop. She's waiting now for him to come back off his honeymoon.

*   *   *

'I hate you, Kelly, and believe me the sooner I never see your ugly face again the better it will be for both of us when we meet again.'

*   *   *

During the war Casey won so many medals the army had to have a firm of decorators in.

*   *   *

The Irish auctioneer shouted, 'The highest bidder will be deemed to be the person or persons nominated as the buyer or buyers unless someone else offers more . . .'

*   *   *

Doctor: 'Well, Mike, I can't quite diagnose your case. I think it must be the drink.'
Michael: 'Shure that's all right, doctor. I know how you feel, I'll come back when you're sober.'

* * *

'This is a very noisy district you live in, Pete!'
'Sure and that's exactly the way it is. We only get any peace at all at all when the heavier trucks drown out the noise.'

* * *

Casey ran to where Riley's poor body lay on the site. 'Are ye dead after such a nasty accident?' he said. 'That I am indeed,' said Riley. 'Faith and you're such a liar I don't know to believe you or not, bejabers.' Riley tried to raise himself and said, 'That proves I'm dead, ye idjit! If I wuz alive you'd not be calling me a liar to me dead face.'

* * *

'Listen to me, Clancy; if Jones comes back before I return tell him I'll meet him at 2 o'clock.' 'Sure I will do that, sor, but what will I tell him if he *doesn't* come?'

* * *

'Want to try my new binoculars, Murph?' Murph tests them. 'H'm that's real magic, Pete, that church across the river is so near I can hear the organ playing.'

*   *   *

Three Irish celebrities wandered into the pub and the spokesman said, 'If it's all right I'll give the orders; three pints of Guinness, wid three pints of export bitter from Dublin, and a half bottle of Mountain Dew Irish whiskey for chasers. Now – what are *you* two havin'?'

*   *   *

'Ye must learn to love your enemies, like the good book says,' thundered the preacher. Rafferty shouted out: 'Oh, I do, I do, your holiness – me worst enemies are whiskey, cigarettes and women!'

*   *   *

The leader of the gang told his members, 'And seeing that it's likely to be a long, hard, cold winter in Fermanagh this year, I tink we best be thievin' them dere houses wid the central heating until de weather improves.'

*   *   *

The political assassin was being hung to death by a committee of his peers and as the executioner came to put the noose round his neck he said, 'Do ye mind usin' a string rope, your honour? – I forgot to tell 'em I'm allergic to nylon.'

*   *   *

Pat O'Donnel spent eight years fighting for his country. And then the owner retired and the Soho bar was closed.

*   *   *

'You must come home and meet de little woman,' Clancy urged, staggering along. When they got there his friend was introduced to a homely woman of some 32 stones, wielding a pick-axe handle.

*   *   *

Daly worked in a busy little bakery and one day his harassed and overworked boss said, 'Quincy, we got trouble. There's so much work the staff can't cope. I'm gonna haveta close down the doughnut section and concentrate on bread.' Quincy said, 'Don't be too hasty, boss: we can manage if you let me do it my way. I'd halve de work by making just da nuts and subcontracting da holes to another factory.'

*   *   *

Clodagh lost her job as an attendant in the Ladies' room of the Club because she kept forgetting the prices.

* * *

The Irish assessor was pushing a policy. He told the prospect, 'And in addition to all de other benefits, if yez smashed up in a terrible accident, we buries you twice.'

* * *

It's an Irish Card Club where everyone plays stud poker. Good players can win as much as 144 collar-studs a night.

* * *

Because Pat had supped too well his host gave him his torch to get home safely because it was a filthy night. About two hours later in the dead of night there is a knock on the host's door and Pat shouts through the letter grille, 'I just came to bring back the torch. I managed to find me way home without it.'

* * *

The designer of the building and the surveyor's assistants finally tied up all the ends, and the go-ahead was given for this 44-storey building. As the whole group trooped out to the nearest pub to celebrate, a small Irishman was noted, standing by the foundation stone which had been blessed a week earlier. 'Don't hang around here, Murphy,' shouted the site boss, 'Be off home wi' ye.'

'Home, nothing,' snorted Murphy. 'You get that lazy crew busy with the scaffolding. I'm waiting to clean the windows.'

* * *

An Irishman went into a music shop and asked for a disc of 'Rhapsody in Blue'. The salesgirl said, 'No, we don't have that on any of our present labels.' The customer says, 'Well just have one more look, miss, perhaps they do it in some other colour.'

* * *

Magistrate: 'Well, I never ever imagined I'd see you again in this Court, Rafferty!'

Rafferty: 'Why's dat, your honour? Was it retiring you was contemplating, sor?'

* * *

Irish Judge: 'The way I see the situation, the *solicitor* is at fault. Paddy O'Brian was not obliged to get wed at all, because according to the evidence the young lady's father had no licence for the rifle in the first place.'

* * *

Inspector: 'O'Grady, what's your game? All those goods there are cheap cotton seconds and you've got them marked "All Wool".'
'Oh, that?' said O'Grady. 'I only do that to fool the moths.'

* * *

Casey came with a barrow-load of very natty ladies' briefs and a broad smile. His business partner asked, 'How can we make a profit with that load of rubbish?' Said Casey, 'I'm after selling them at the disco and the Go-Go girls can have 'em at rock-bottom prices.'

* * *

'Shaun, can you understand this French on the label?'
'Yes, so long as it's written in Irish.'

* * *

'Drink is a curse,' proclaimed the Irish minister, 'It makes you quarrel with your neighbour, and shoot at your landlord . . . and miss . . .'

* * *

After the affray, the Irish judge roared, 'Any fool who maliciously sets fire to a barn to burn it in addition to burning a stable full of horses ought to be kicked to death by an imbecile jackass and I'd like to be the one to do it.'

*　　*　　*

Chairman of the bench: 'We find the man who stole the horse which scattered the chickens and caused the dog to chase the bull through Mr James' window, not guilty.'

*　　*　　*

Riley was waylaid on the way home.
'Your money or your life,' snarled the robber.
Said Riley, 'Then yez best be taking me life, sor, as I'm saving me money for me old age.'

*　　*　　*

Magistrates' Court: 'You're here again, I see, Shaun Sweeney.'
'Yes, your honour.'
'What brings you here this time, my lad?'
'It was a couple of gentlemen police officers, your highness.'
'Drunk to a coma, I suppose?'
'Yes, your worship, especially the one wid the side-boards.'

*　　*　　*

'What does I tink of Casey? I'll tell you exactly what I tink. He's one of those that pat you on the back in front of your face and hit you in the mouth behind your back. Begorrah.'

* * *

'Did your mother come from Ireland?'
'Yes. Well, she had to. There was no-one else to stoke the boiler, 'cos the captain had a hernia.'

* * *

'Has anyone here seen me vest, then?'
'Shure and you have the thing on, you fool.'
'Well tanks anyway because I'd have gone without it if you hadn't happen to notice.'

* * *

I'm dead tired this morning . . . I had to wait up for the cat so I could put him out and he didn't come home till 3 a.m.

* * *

'You *are* a mechanic, ain't you, Shaun?'
'Not at all, I'm a MacArthur. The McAnnex are my sister's side of the family.'

* * *

A gang of workmen fresh from the emerald isle were sent to measure a GPO post by the telephone manager. Unfortunately their ladder was too short. 'Roight, den,' shouted the foreman, 'we'll have to be laying it down on the ground to measure it.' One of the gang shouted back, 'Don't be daft, it's the height we're needing, not the bloody breadth.'

* * *

The foreman on a building site was showing prospective buyers around the new estate. 'Here are de walls built by the foinest Irish brickies,' he told the visitors. Then he shouted outside through the window, 'Green side up!' He showed them the staircase. 'Built by the foinest Irish chippies,' he said, then went to the window and shouted down, 'Hoi, green sides up.' Then he showed them the bathroom fittings and shouted through the window to the men below, 'Green side up.' One potential house-buyer asked the foreman, 'Why do you keep shouting through the windows?' The foreman said, 'Down dere are de foinest Irish gardeners in de world, laying the lawns.'

* * *

The reason why Irish setter dogs have flattened noses is because they spend a lot of their time chasing parked Jaguars.

* * *

Shamus joined a robber band and on the night of his first safe-cracking job the boss warned him, 'Before we goes trough de window, you put on your tights and stretch 'em right over your face, get it?' But Shamus went on the job unmasked. The boss roared, 'Didn't I tell you to stretch some tights over your face, you crumb!' Shamus said, 'Sure and you can see for yourself that the daft things will only stretch as high as me neck!'

* * *

Shamus to Mike: 'What happens if the bomb goes off in the boot?'
Mike: 'Stop worrying. There's another in the engine.'

* * *

Paddy: My girlfriend doesn't believe in banks. She keeps all her money in her brassiere.
Mick: Why her brassiere?
Paddy: It draws more interest there.

* * *

Three Irishmen kidnapped Dr Kissinger, and sent him home to New York with a ransom note pinned to his dicky.

* * *

Paddy bought himself a paper shop in Belfast . . . and the wind blew it away.

*   *   *

An Irish terrorist switched off the fans of his stolen helicopter because the draught was unbearable.

*   *   *

Paddy won two prizes in the 'Generation Game' on TV . . . a pair of swing doors and a conveyor belt.

*   *   *

An old Mick picking his toes in a Sauna took the lining right out of his wellies.

*   *   *

An Irish labourer got himself a job sweeping the leaves on a Stately Estate – and fell out of the tree. Fortunately he didn't break anything important as he landed on his head.

*   *   *

Paddy bought a new pair of wellies from Freeman Hardy and Willis and complained that he didn't like third-hand footwear even if it was for his feet. Anyway, he added, the string needs lengthening.

*   *   *

Taffy has entered for the next Olympics – Heading the Shot and Catching the Javelin.

*   *   *

Paddy was temporarily out of work and the Exchange sent him for a part-time position with a building company. Last seen he was climbing up a seventy-foot ladder with a hod full of Lego.

*   *   *

An Irish applicant for a teaching job at Cambridge was asked questions on Greek Mythology. 'Which creature was half a man and half a beast?' Paddy said, 'Would that be Buffalo Bill?'

*   *   *

Mike's wife asked for a fur coat for her birthday and she got a double-breasted donkey jacket.

*   *   *

With so many immigrants moving from Ireland into Holland the Dutch are busy turning out thousands of pairs of pinewood wellies. Hundreds of various factories are now clogging on and clogging off daily.

*   *   *

Paddy became an entertainer and at a Scottish theatre one night they begged him to do something typically Irish – so he demolished the theatre roof and dug up the car park.

*   *   *

Paddy jumped off a high tower on the building site and smashed both his legs. When he regained consciousness, two years later, he said: 'That's funny, my Dad flew Wellingtons during the war, and never got more than a few bits of flak in his head.'

*   *   *

Why are there camels in Saudi Arabia and Irish labourers in London?
That's easy – the Arabs had first choice.

*   *   *

Ground Control to Aer Lingus Flight 233, please give us your height and exact position . . . Aer Lingus pilot shouts back, 'I'm five feet five in my rubbers, and I'm sitting in the driving seat alongside my parachute and an inflatable rubber thingy.'

*   *   *

The control tower demanded, 'Are you sure you're the captain of that aircraft?' and Paddy replied, 'How else would I get three gold rings round my wellies?'

*   *   *

Mike fell down a Wishing Well at Rhyl. His friend shouted down, 'Are you hurt? Anything broken?' and Mike shouted back, 'No, look you, there's nothing down here to break.'

*　　*　　*

An Irish visitor noticed an attractive young girl standing under a lamp-post and chatted her. 'Do you know what you remind me of,' he said, 'standing there all dressed in red?'
'No. What?' she said.
'An omnibus,' he said.
She said: 'Get lost! Don't think you're getting a ride on ME for ten cents.'

*　　*　　*

He's earning a fortune forging period furniture, working from plans in a Do-It-Thyself handbook.

*　　*　　*

What do you get if you cross an Irishman with a sow?
Thick Bacon.

*　　*　　*

What do you get if you cross a London nude-runner with a pig?
Streaker bacon.

*　　*　　*

What do you call an Irish brain surgeon? A chiropodist.

*　　*　　*

What's blackened, all shrivelled up and hangs from a ceiling? An Irish electric mechanic.

*　　*　　*

What do they call an Irish rabbi who rushes around town circumcising everyone in sight? A kliptomaniac.

*　　*　　*

How can you make an Irishman dizzy? Put him in an empty oil barrel and tell him to wee in the corner.

*　　*　　*

How can you make an Irish farmhand burn his right ear? Phone him while he's ironing his trousers.

*　　*　　*